Is baby Jesus in Heaven?

Is baby Jesus at home in Nazareth?

Is he with the shepherds?

Is baby Jesus with the angels?

Is baby Jesus with
the wise men?

Is baby Jesus at King Herod's palace?

Is baby Jesus at the inn?

Is baby Jesus with the children?

Is baby Jesus
in the stable?

Where is baby Jesus now?